CHAT-U

AND PUT DOWNS

STEWART FERRIS

SUMMERSDALE

Summersdale Publishers
46 West Street
Chichester
West Sussex
PO19 1RP
England

ISBN 1 84024 020 2

Printed in Great Britain.

A CIP catalogue record for this book is available from the British Library.

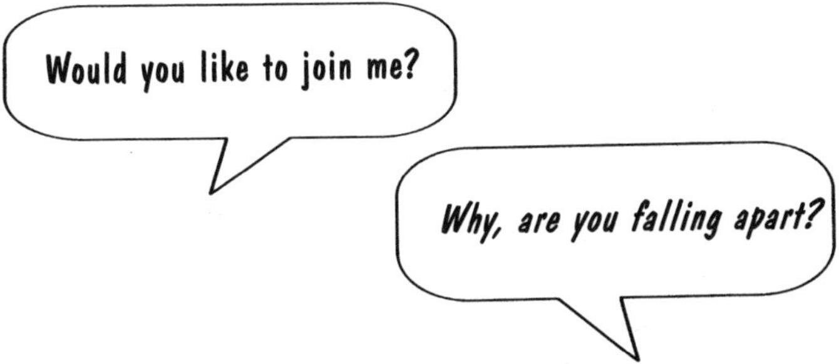
Would you like to join me?
Why, are you falling apart?

Would you like to come and meet my family?

OK, when are the opening hours?

Is that a gun in your pocket or are you just pleased to see me?

No, it's a gun.

I'd like to take you out to eat.

Why won't you eat me indoors?

What would it take to get a little kiss from you?

Chloroform.

Hello, I'm a stamp collector.

Well you're not mounting me.

Do you have a favourite singer?

Yes, the one with two bobbins and a foot pedal.

There's a woman like you in my dreams every night.

I hope she can swim.

My friends told me all about you.

What friends?

Hi there. I'd like to ask you what's your idea
of a perfect evening?

> *The one I was having before you came over.*

I'm a musician. I'm famous for what I can do with my
little piccolo.

> *That's nice. Did you say you were a musician as well?*

I'm a meteorologist, and I'd like to study your warm front. Let's go to an isobar and have a drink.

No thanks — I've seen the forecast. Damp in parts, hot and sticky with rising cumulo nimbus. I think I'll stay at home.

My ideal woman has to have a great sense of humour.

That will have to be the only sense she has.

You've got the face of an angel.

And you've got the face of a saint
— a Saint Bernard.

You're the best looking bloke I've ever seen.

Thanks, I wish I could say the same for you.

You could if you were as big a liar as me.

Am I the first person who has ever tried to seduce you?

You could be — your face looks familiar.

Which part of my bed would you like to sleep on?

The top bunk.

I've just been to the doctor. I thought I
had acute angina, but he said I was
imagining it.

No, no, he's wrong
— it's gorgeous.

What would you give me if I agreed to sleep with you?

Syphilis.

I love your crazy hair — it looks like
you've got grass growing out of it.

*That's odd
— I planted tulips.*

You look like you haven't changed your
shirt in a fortnight.

That's impossible — I've only had it a week.

I'm a magician. Would you like me to perform
a spell for you?

OK, can you make yourself disappear?

I've come from another planet to seek out
beautiful life forms.

Is that because your race is so ugly?

I want people to love me for myself, not my money.

Isn't that narrowing your options somewhat?

Can I introduce you to my dog, Raffles?

> *Oh, isn't he big? Can I stroke him?*

Of course. Would you like to stroke Raffles as well?

God ordered me to come to you.

> *What's He up to? That's the fifth one this week.*
> *I've sent all the others back.*

I never forget a face.

Neither do I, but in your case I'll make an exception.

Can I have a tinkle on your piano?

I'd rather you used the toilet.

Are your legs tired? You've been running through my mind all day.

Yeh — I was looking for a brain cell.

Do you want to know why I'm feeling sad?

There's no reason, you're just sad.

I climb mountains for a hobby, but getting
on top of you is probably going to be my
biggest challenge to date.

That depends on the length of your rope.

If you should happen to fall in love with me,
I'll be waiting for you.

If I ever get that desperate I won't be worth waiting for.

I saw your face in the reflection of the moonlight
on the lake last night.

No you didn't.

20

Try imagining you're in love with me.

My imagination doesn't stretch that far.

The name's Thomas, John Thomas.

That's OK, I'm Holly, so I'm used to little pricks.

Would you go to bed with a perfect stranger?

                            Yes — but you're not perfect.

Don't go away — I'm just going to put the kettle on.

                            Are you sure it will fit you?

When can we be alone?

        When we're not with each other.

Kiss me quick.

        Don't you fancy me enough to kiss me slowly?

It's great that we met here tonight.
Why don't we meet up again?

Because I don't want to.

Don't you think that a man's charisma
is more important than the size of
his penis?

But you've got hardly any charisma either.

Shall we go and see a film?

I've seen it.

Do you think you could fall for me?

Only if you pushed me.

May I introduce myself?

Certainly — try those people over there.

Am I your dream come true?

I don't know yet. Go and stand in the road
with your eyes closed, and we'll see.

You must tell me your name.

It begins with 'Mrs'. Shall I bother to continue?

If I had known I was going to meet someone as amazingly lovely as you, I'd have had my nostrils plucked.

And if I'd known I was going to meet someone as ugly as you, I'd have had my eyeballs plucked.

Do you think it was fate that brought us together?

No. It was just bad luck.

Would you like to come out with me for some coq au vin?

What sort of van do you drive?

When I roll across my satin sheets at
night, the sound reminds me of you.

What, while I'm eating a packet of crisps?

When I look at the stars I see your eyes. When
I look at a flower I smell your perfume. When I
look at the sun I feel your warmth.

When I look at a cow I see your bullshit.

I've heard you're a good cook, but there is
no recipe for my love for you.

What about Mini Sausages with Leeks?

30

Look, to decide whether or not we should date, let's toss for it.

No, let's just flip a coin. Heads — you don't get to go out with me, tails — I don't get to go out with you. Fair?

What would you say is my best feature?

Your ornamental pond.

I'm considering chucking my girlfriend
for you. How do you feel about that?

But I don't want your girlfriend.

Don't go — you'll never find anyone like me again.

I certainly hope not.

Where can I find mutual love?

At the beginning of a tennis match.

My stars said I would meet the woman of my dreams tonight.

I'll go and see if I can find her for you.

Where can we go from here?

I don't care, so long as you go first.

Can I have your name?

Why — haven't you already got one?

It's OK, we can be together tonight. I've given my girlfriend the evening off.

What for, good behaviour?

I've always believed in love at first sight.

So did I — until I met you.

I've lost my script, so we'll have to ad-lib.

I don't think much of your part, anyway.

Can I kiss you?

Of course, but mind you don't burn yourself on my cigarette.

Do you mind if I smoke?

I don't care if you burn.

I'm sure I could turn you on.

You couldn't even turn on a radio.

Hello. Didn't we sleep together once? Or was it twice?

It must have been once. I never make the same mistake twice.

You seem to me like a sensible girl.

That's right — I won't go anywhere near you.

You would be great to go on a camping holiday with.
Separate tents, of course.

I'd prefer separate campsites.

Would you like a nibble of my sausage?

Not yet. Let's eat first.

Do I get the impression that you're playing hard to get?

No, I'm playing impossible to get.

I've got some condoms, so I think
we should sleep together right now.

What's the hurry? Are they close to their expiry date?

Do you come here often?

Not if you do.

You're very pretty, but your eyes indicate
you've had a sheltered life.

> *They've only been sheltering from you.*

Do you kiss with your eyes closed?

> *I would if I were kissing you.*

Hey, you're not much of a looker, but I'll have you.

Thanks. You must be very open-minded.
Was that how your brain slipped out?

Oi, darling, do you want to really enjoy yourself with me?

Sorry, I couldn't possibly entertain the thought of
spending time with someone who splits infinitives.

No, I'll pay for you as well.

Shall we go all the way?

> Yes, as long as it's in different directions.

Would you accept if I were to ask you out?

> Accept what — defeat?

You don't sweat much for a fat lass.

       I will when I start running away from you.

I had no idea I would ever meet someone like you in here.

*I had no idea they would ever **let** someone like you in here.*

I'd like to see more of you.

There isn't any more of me.

I think I could make you very happy.

Why, are you leaving?

It's funny, I know I'm a bit drunk, well, very drunk, but I'm sure I know you from somewhere. Any chance of a kiss?

Hello Dad.

Hi. I'm a tenor.

Sorry, I've only got a fiver.

Go on, don't be shy: ask me out.

OK, get out.

What happened to your face? Do you step on rakes for a hobby?

No, I impersonate you.

Didn't we used to be lovers?

Yes. I left you because you have an infuriating memory problem.

I don't remember that.

You have a peach-like complexion
— pale and wrinkly.

>   *You don't look like a peach, but your breath smells as if*
>   *you've been eating them. A week ago.*

Your face is familiar — I might even say commonplace.

>   *Yours must have been a limited edition —*
>   *limited because no one else wanted one like it.*

Your face is absolutely perfect.

> *So is yours . . . for radio.*

You're the kind of girl I'd like to take home
to mother except I can't trust my father.

> *Don't worry — he's not the sort
> to drink from the same cup twice.*

You've got everything a man could want:
teeth, hair, moustache . . .

All I lack is your charm and subtlety.

Will you come out with me on Saturday?

Sorry, I'm having a headache at the weekend.

Can I have your phone number?

        No, but you can have my dialling code.

Would you mind if I take a lock of your hair?

        Why, are you trying to stuff a mattress?

Where did you get those big blue eyes?

They came with my face.

You're just my type — you're a girl.

I'm just my type as well, I'm afraid.

You look like my fourth wife.

How many have you had?

Three.

56

I'm not interested in a relationship,
but I don't feel like being alone tonight.

Are you asking for a shag, or what?

You must be a Mars bar, because I'm
a chocoholic and I want you badly.

You're certainly doing badly.

I haven't done this sort of thing before. I want you to teach me.

> OK, you go out of that door, close
> it gently behind you, and go away.

Shall we go somewhere quieter?

> No need — I've got some earmuffs you can borrow.

I'd go to the ends of the world for you.

Yes, but would you stay there?

Please talk to me so that creep over there will leave me alone.

I just said that to someone about you.

Shall I tell you my name?

Why?

So you'll know what to scream.

May I have a drag on your fag?

That's ironic — actually I am a fag in drag.

Let's skip the awkward beginning and pretend that we have known each other for a while. So, how's your Mum?

She told me I wasn't to see you any more.

You look like a model.

No, I'm real.

You've got a smile that could light up a whole town.

You've got a mouth that could accommodate a whole town.

You're so hot you melt the elastic in my underwear.

I wondered what the smell was.

What would you say if I asked you to marry me?

Nothing. I can't talk and laugh at the same time.

Listen, I want to tell you something . . .
I'm not wearing any underwear.

*Don't worry — there's a shop just round
the corner where you can get some.*

I miss my teddy bear. Will you sleep with me?

Here, borrow mine.

Is it hot in here or is it just you?

It's hot.

Is your daddy a thief?

No.

Then how did he steal the stars
out of the sky and put them in your eyes?

Is your daddy a thief?

Yes.

Can he get me a cheap video?

I like every muscle in my body. Especially yours.

What's a girl like you doing in a nice place like this?

Hey, don't I know you?

Not yet. Ask me another.

67

Do you know what would look good on you?

No?

Me.

Going my way? Can I walk with you?

You can walk near me.

If I told you that you have a beautiful body,
would you hold it against me?

No, I'd just hit you.

How about coming back to my place for a
bit of heavy breathing?

Why, is the lift broken?

Do you know where we are?

Why?

Because I'm lost in your eyes.

Do you have the number for heaven?

Why?

It looks like they've lost an angel.

Where shall we go for our honeymoon?

    What about Finland? And I'll go to New Zealand.

Will you join me in a glass of wine?

    I don't think there'd be room for both of us.

Can I borrow ten pence? I want to call my
mother and thank her.

I'd complain if I were you.

Can I have directions?

To where?

To your heart.

Feel a muscle, any muscle.

All these curves, and me with no brakes.

Can I borrow your phone?

Why?

My ex told me to call when I fell in love again.

Can I flirt with you?

I was hoping to meet someone a little younger.
People might think you're my mother.

I'd like to take you to dinner.

Sure — can you pick me up again afterwards?

Good evening. I'm conducting research to find my ideal partner, and I'd like to ask you a couple of questions: will you come to bed with me, and if so how much do you charge?

Yes, I'll go to bed with you, and I don't normally charge, but for you I'd make an exception.

Do you get out of the bath to go
to the toilet?

No need — I bathe in the toilet.

Where is the toilet?

Oh, I didn't realise you were house trained.

You probably think I'm mad coming up to you like this, but I have this strange urge to buy you a drink.

I don't want anything to do with your strange urges.

Weren't you at the party last week?

Yes. And I haven't changed my mind since then, I'm afraid.

I'm afraid I'm an incurable romantic.

Well, you're incurable, that's for sure.

I've waited all my life to meet you.

Stuck at the back of the queue, were you?

Virtually everyone here is ugly except you.

> *Well you're so ugly I bet your psychiatrist*
> *makes you lie face down on the couch.*

Very difficult getting served here.
What are you having in case I get served first?

> *An attack of nausea.*

Most guys are like public toilets; either vacant,
engaged or full of crap. Which are you?

Er, could you repeat the question?

Kiss me.

You'll have to drug me first.

Will you sleep with me.

No, I'm an insomniac.

What would you do if you ever got chatted-up by a woman?

Warn her that I used to be one.

The trouble with this place is some
of the people that come here.

Do something about it — leave.

Shall we introduce ourselves?

        I already know myself. What about you?

You'd look good in anything but the mirror.

        At least I've got a mirror.

Ring me sometime. Must dash now, but here's my number.

Don't you have a name?

Shall we share a taxi to the nightclub?

I wouldn't even share the earth with you if I had a choice.

Queuing is so boring, don't you find?

It is now.

Please take a seat.

Where to?

'Yes' is my favourite word. What's yours?

No.

How did you get to be so beautiful?

I must have been given your share.

On a scale of one to ten, you have been voted ten by everyone over there. How do you feel?

I use my fingertips.

Can you give me your name, please?

I don't think 'Melissa' would suit you.

Nobody I know can tell me who you are,
but I'm sure I've seen you before.

*Why don't you take that ugly mask off so that I
can see what you look like?*

No, don't tell me: you're a Pisces?

OK, I won't tell you.

Very nice gear you've got on.

Yeh, and it's staying on.

Quick, the lights are coming back on in a minute. Kiss me.

No. I'm your wife.

I love your hair.

Which one?

My friend fancies you.

You just keep your friend in his underpants, out of trouble.

May I have the pleasure of this dance?

No, I'd like some pleasure too.

I don't normally do this sort of thing, but here's my card — I'd like to meet you some time.

You just did.

Keep it up — you're doing well.

I wish I could say the same for you.

Life has been empty without you.

I'm not letting you fill me up.

Isn't it boring here? Do you want to go somewhere else?

You go — that will be enough to liven things up.

Are you sisters?

Yes.

You must have left Cinderella at home.

I'm raising money for charity by charging for kisses.

Never mind the kisses, just take the money.

I've been given a couple of tickets for the play on Thursday —
do you want to come?

Only if you give me both of them.

I don't suppose you would be interested in going
out one night to see a film?

I'm already booked that night.

I'm a doctor: what's your appendix doing tonight? I'd love to take it out.

Very funny. You should be on the television — then I could turn you off.

Going so soon? Stay a minute and let me get you a drink.

Just give me the cash — I'll get one later.

Fancy a swim?

*I can't swim, so shall we jump straight
to the bit where you resuscitate me?*

Got a light?

Yes thanks.

Um, hello.

Oscar Wilde, I presume?

Every time I come here I've seen you.
I'd like to know more about you.

So would the police.

Forgive me for being so forward, but I
think I love you.

*Come back and see me when
you're certain.*

Don't drink the beer here. It's awful. Try my saliva instead.

Got any nuts?

Do you like my new jacket?

It's great. Shame your body doesn't suit it, though.

Can I buy you a drink?

I would think so — why don't you ask the barman?

Can you microwave this?

Yes, but it will be too hot to wear afterwards.

Excuse me: I don't normally talk to strange women in the street, but I'm on my way to confession and I'm a bit short of material.

Try the draper's shop.

I always swallow.

Good. You'd starve otherwise.

Let's eat out. How about Japanese?

> *I'm a bit short-sighted, so don't have the raw
> fish, or I won't know which end of you is which.*

What's the biggest problem in your life?

> *Look in a mirror.*

I've forgotten your name but I'll never forget your face. I'm reminded of it every morning when I hop on the back of the bus.

Why would you hop on a bus? Wouldn't it be easier to use both legs?

Have you ever tried drinking Australian wine?

What else would I be doing with it?

I've seen your beautiful face before, I'm sure.

Yes, I'm a friend of your wife's.

I'm fat, I'm ugly, I'm hairy, I'm smelly, and I fart like a wind tunnel. But I'm bloody rich.

I don't want you thinking I'm just after your money, darling. What's your name?

You show me yours, I'll show you mine.

OK, my boyfriend's over there.

Do you take the washing-up out of the sink
before you piss into it?

No. Nor after.

Hi. I'm on a computer date, actually, but the computer hasn't shown up. Do you want to join me instead?

No, I never date men with tiny peripherals.

Er, hello. My name's, er . . . I can't remember.

That's a lovely name.

I like the way you dye your roots brown.

At least I've got roots.

What do you think of the music here?

Better than the company.

Umpteen people must have already told you this,
but you're very beautiful.

You're so ugly, Frankenstein's Monster would go to a
Halloween party as you.

You know what I like most about you? All of you.

> *That's great, because I'm an all or nothing*
> *sort of person, and with you it's nothing.*

I'd like to cook for you — I'm a great cook.

> *No thanks, I'm not much of an eater.*

Hello.

Goodbye.

Have you got a problem with that?

No, only with you.

Have you got any Irish in you?

                                                            No.

Would you like some?

                                Yes please. Mine's a Guinness.

Cheer up darling, it may never happen.

                                                    It just has.

Can you see me in your future?

No. You're already in my past.

With you I've finally found what I've been looking for in life.

With you I've finally lost it.

Kiss me and I'll tell you a secret.

I know your secret - I work at the clinic.

How do you keep an idiot in suspense?

Don't know.

Nor me. Been waiting for someone to tell me, actually.

Would you like another drink?

Do you really think our relationship will last that long?

Have you ever done it with a real man?

No, why - have you?

Are you happy?

I was.

If I could dance, I'd ask you to dance, but I can't.
If I could sail, I'd take you sailing, but I can't.
However, I'm the father of twelve kids. How about it?

Would you like my ship to sail into your port?

No. It's an airport.

Haven't I seen your face before — on a police poster?

Look who's talking — I bet when you go to the zoo you have to buy two tickets: one to get in and another to get out.

When will we meet again?

In another life, I hope.

Are you separated?

No, it's just the way I walk.

Do you know what I am?

A eunuch?

Are you a miner?

No.

Oh, so that's not a pickaxe in your pocket?

How would you like your eggs in the morning?

Unfertilised, mate. Piss off.

What's your favourite record?

Sebastion Coe's 1500 metres.

I'm a photographer for a model agency:
I've been looking for a face like yours.

I'm a plastic surgeon.
I've been looking for a face like yours.

I drive a Formula One racing car.

So why were you late?

I work in the music business.

I know, I've been to your shop.

What's your favourite film?

Kodak.

I've circumnavigated the world single-handed.

What were you doing with your other hand, then?

What's your favourite flower?

Self-raising.

How can I prove my love for you?

In a court of law.

Do you believe in sex before marriage?

In general, yes, but with you I'd make an exception.

Do you fancy coming for a walk in the woods?

What for — to meet your family?

I want people to like me for what I am.

Is that why you drive a Porsche?

What's your favourite French dish?

Gerard Depardieu.

Have you had a wonderful evening?

Sure, but it wasn't this one.

Other Humour Books from Summersdale

How To Chat-up Women
Stewart Ferris   £4.99

How To Chat-up Men
Amy Mandeville   £4.99

How To Stay Married
Dick Hills   £4.99

500 Chat-up Lines and Put Downs
Stewart Ferris   £4.99

101 Uses for a Losing Lottery Ticket
Shovel/Nadler   £3.99

101 Ways To Spend Your Lottery Millions
Jenny Humphreys   £3.99

Men! Can't Live with them, Can't live with them
Tania Golightly   £3.99

Girl Power
Kitty Malone   £3.99

The Kama Sutra For One
O'Nan and P. Palm   £3.99

Paws For Thought:
Another Purrfect Day   £3.99

Paws For Thought:
It's A Dog's Life   £3.99

Available from all good bookshops.